The Big Yellow House on Grandfather's Farm

THE JOURNEY

Agnes Evans Gish

HERITAGE BOOKS
2018

HERITAGE BOOKS
AN IMPRINT OF HERITAGE BOOKS, INC.

Books, CDs, and more—Worldwide

For our listing of thousands of titles see our website
at
www.HeritageBooks.com

Published 2018 by
HERITAGE BOOKS, INC.
Publishing Division
5810 Ruatan Street
Berwyn Heights, Md. 20740

Copyright © 2018 Agnes Evans Gish

Heritage Books by the author:

The Big Yellow House on Grandfather's Farm: The Journey
The Big Yellow House on Grandfather's Farm: Cousin Lillian Comes to the Farm
The Sweet Springs of Western Virginia: a Bittersweet Legacy
Virginia Taverns, Ordinaries and Coffee Houses:
18th–Early 19th Century Entertainment Along the Buckingham Road

All rights reserved. No part of this book may be reproduced or transmitted in any form or by any means, electronic or mechanical, including photocopying, recording or by any information storage and retrieval system without written permission from the author, except for the inclusion of brief quotations in a review.

International Standard Book Numbers
Paperbound: 978-0-7884-5799-9

I DEDICATE THIS BOOK

to

MY IMMIGRANT HERITAGE

My Mother

Stephanie Frödl Evans

and

My Grandparents

Theresa Bednar Frödl and Vincent Frödl

who arrived in America in 1899

from the villages of

Jamne nad Orlici and Damníkov (Thomigsdorf),

then Bohemia, now Present Czech Republic

To all who helped to make this book possible,

Thank You!

Cousin Lillian Kotasek Simonelli,

Julie Gish Norris and Gregory Pastor,

Gina Warren Buzby, Carol Campbell, Kathy Byus

Thelma Mrazek and Mary Dulany

PROLOGUE: HISTORICAL BACKGROUND

At the turn of the Twentieth Century, a vast wave of Eastern Europeans immigrated to America to settle in its heartland. The author's grandparents were among those who migrated first to North Dakota, then Wisconsin, and finally to Nebraska. Grandfather who was German in name, came from the small village of Thomigsdorf near the Austrian border. His ancestors were sent from Frankfurt, to teach the natives how to farm. Grandmother came from the village of Jamné, closer to Prague. Grandfather arrived first in order to find work and then send for his bride-to-be. They were married in Wisconsin at the home of relatives. Grandfather worked in the Cudahy meat-packing business, but the cold and dampness crippled him. It was then that destiny brought to his attention a sleepy little town surrounded by idle plantation land that once thrived in cotton and peanuts in southern Virginia.

Thirty-seven years after the Civil War put an end to the use of slaves to till those fields, Col. Henry W. Weiss of Emporia, Virginia, devised a scheme to sell land in smaller tracts to those nationalities adept in small farming, namely Czech, German, Russian and Polish. To attract these buyers, Col. Weiss published an advertising sheet, called "*The Virginian*" which he distributed in the northern states, where so many from the "Old Country" had come to settle. To accommodate visitors to his properties, he opened a hotel on Emporia's Main Street.

Vincent Frödl, the author's grandfather, was one who came across a copy of the advertisement. A warm climate would be beneficial, his doctor concurred, so to look at those properties, he boarded the train headed east to Grand Central Station in New York to connect with the train headed south.

After viewing several parcels shown to him by Col. Weiss, Mr. Frödl picked out one hundred acres, equidistant between the towns of Jarratt and Emporia. Within nine years, Mr. Frödl's farm prospered. He paid off his loan, renounced his allegiance to Francis Joseph, Emperor of Austria, and became an American citizen.

TRANSLATIONS

Agnes' grandparents used certain foreign words and phrases when speaking to her. Her grandmother, a native of Bohemia - present day Czech Republic - spoke Czech. Her grandfather, although he too came from Bohemia, spoke German. His village "Damníkov," ("Thomigsdorf"), near Austria's border, was inhabited solely by Germans. Early in the settlement of this Czech-speaking country, his forebears, natives of Frankfurt, Germany, were sent there to teach the natives how to farm.

CZECH: *Anežka* – [Ah-neyesh-kah] - Agnes

Kolache – [ko- la- chee] – Cakes or cookies

GERMAN : *Frödl,* the name rhymes with "yodel"

Enklein-[enk-keh- lin] grandchild

Guten morgen [goo-ten mor-ghen] – Good morning

Herr Hase [hair hah-za] Mister Rabbit

Kommen sie, Kind [comin' see kindt] – Come here, child

Mach schnell [mock schnell] - Make it quick *Mädchen* [made- chin] – Little girl

HOW TO READ ALOUD EFFECTIVELY

◆ Familiarize yourself with the pronunciations of the Czech and German words and phrases found under Translations.

◆ Read rhythmically. The text is written in poetic *iambic* meter wherein stress is placed on the second beat of the spoken word:

. / . / . / - ta DUM   ta DUM   ta DUM

    Ex. The **train** from New **York**

◆ Encourage participation in reciting the repetitious phrase

    Ex. The Big Yellow House on Grandfather's Farm.

◆ Look for sound words like *squeak* and *swish.*

◆ Color the tone of your voice. When you read the little girl's answer to the mailman, try a soft pink and for the mailman, a dark brown.

◆ Vary your pitch. A field mouse would sound shrill compared to a honking goose.

◆ Vary your pace. The text describing a tired child passing rows and rows of crops should be read slowly with lackluster.

◆ For groups of children: at the Ruckus, let each child assume an animal character's voice. Imagine their cacophonous sound as they attempt to sing the closing lines of the story in animal-speak:

    "We're glad that you've come to the

    BIG YELLOW HOUSE ON GRANDFATHER'S FARM."

Have fun!

Create a Ruckus!

The Big Yellow House on Grandfather's Farm

THE JOURNEY

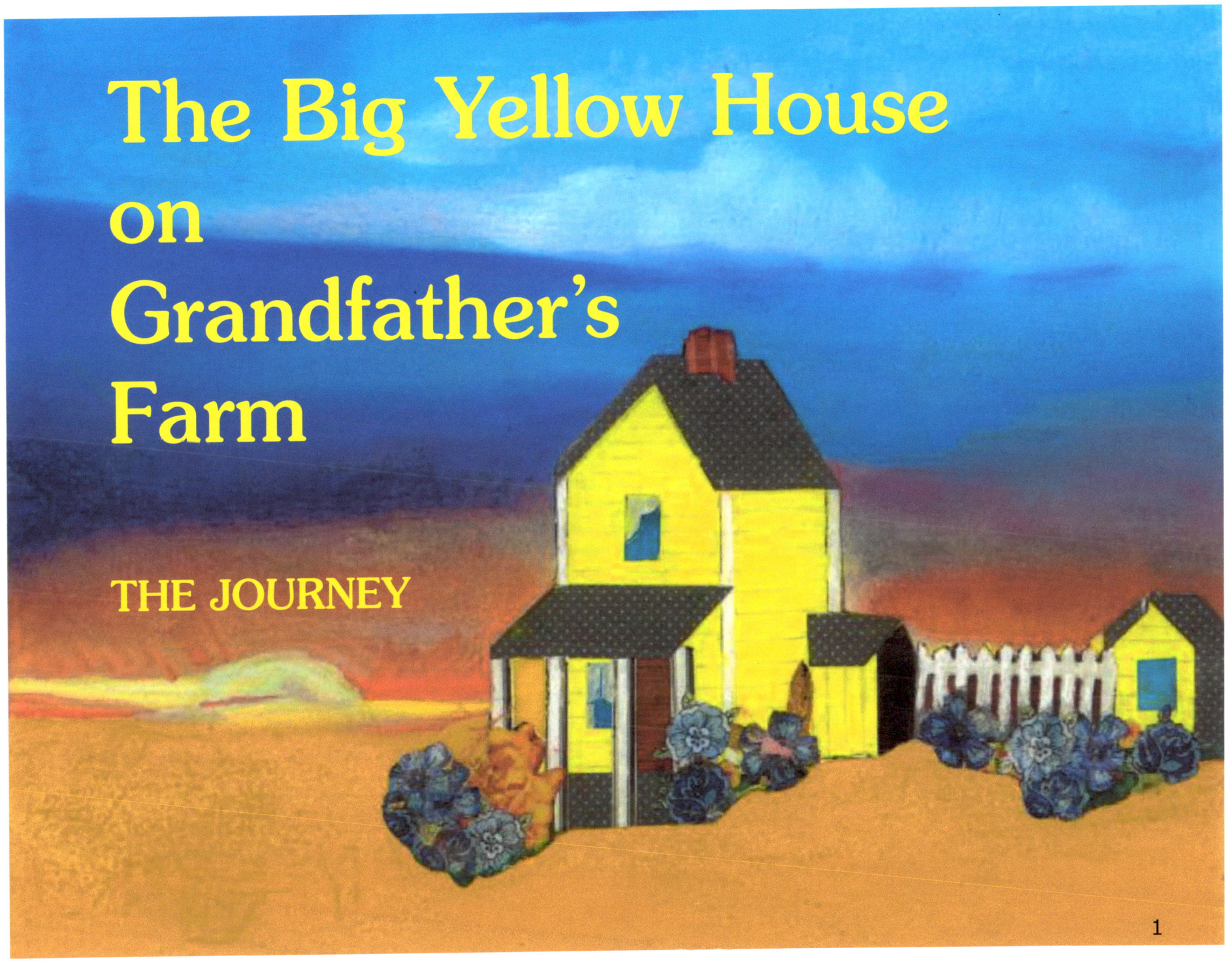

Drawings by the author based on memory and a few faded family photographs in her possession.

Mid puffs
of
white smoke,
the train
from
New York

idled at
Emporia's station.

Inside the coach, a sleeping child woke.
"Emporia? That's my destination!"

Gathering her things
she clambered in haste
down the steps of the train
to the platform.

Peering around the southern town,
she searched for the mailman,
Mister Owen.

"He is the one",
Mother had said,
"Who will take you to where you are goin'."

"Hello, little girl," Mr. Owen called out, "Are you the one going to Frödl's?"

Shyly, she answered, "I'm going home to the Big Yellow House on Grandfather's Farm."

They drove many miles
down the dusty dirt road
'til they came to
her grandfather's mailbox.

He helped her get out,
pointed the way,
then drove off
to finish his mail route.

She passed rows of peanuts.

She passed rows of corn.

She passed rows of cotton.
"Whew! What a big farm!"

Tired, she sat beneath a shade tree. "S-q-u-e-a-k, S-q-u-e-a-k" broke the silence. She looked down to see from whence came the squeaking.

"It's coming from me!" said a tiny grey field mouse, "A field mouse?" gasped she. "A field mouse I am, I am, yes-sir-ee!"

"Grandfather sent me," said the little grey mouse,
"To show you the rest of the way to his house."

He bowed and then
he puffed out
his wee mousy chest.
"Look down the road
beyond the next crest."

There in the light of the sun going down,
The Big Yellow House on Grandfather's Farm!

Grandfather near crushed her within his embrace. His handlebar moustache tickled her face.

"*Anežka*," said Grandmother, with a big hug. "For you, warm *koláč*, cool milk from the jug."

Her tummy near bustin', the little girl said,
"Please Grandma, I'm tired. May I go to bed?"

The rain on the tin of the roof overhead
soon lulled her to sleep in the downy-soft bed.

She woke up next morning
to rooster's loud crow:

"Time to get up!
the sky's all aglow!"

She jumped out of bed,
but instead of her dress,
a pair of blue overalls
lay on the chest.

She scarcely had put on
the big overalls,
when up the steep stairway
she heard Grandpa call.

"*Kommen sie, kind,*" her grandfather said. "Each day chores must be done, livestock fed."

With her hand in his, they made their way down to the corn crib with baskets to fill up with corn.

They fed first
the cows,
then filled up
the horse trough
with corn
from the crib,
sweet hay
from the loft.

He next harnessed Daisy, "Where are we going?"
"The garden," he answered, "It needs hours of plowing."

So up rows of green things, old Daisy's hooves plod
to wrap up earth's blanket round roots
snug and good.

Once finished with plowing,
he lifted her down
by the hutch
where White Rabbit lived
close to the ground.

*"Guten Morgen,
Herr Hase,*
I want you to meet
Meine Enkelin Agnes
with lettuce to eat."

The white rabbit nibbled,
then flopped one long ear,
"Thank you, dear Agnes.
I'm glad you are here."

With these chores
all finished,
he took her to meet
the tiny wee things
that 'round a farm creep.

For down by the
hen house
some ducklings
she spied
paddling in a puddle.
"Quack, quack,"
they began.

"What fun you'll have
with us!" Then away
they all ran.

"Cluck, cluck,"
said the Red Hen
strutting her charm as
she gathered her chicks
under wings nice and warm.

A big goose honked noisily,
"My goslings, when grown
will give you their feathers
for soft pillow-down."

Hearing loud grunting, she ran just beyond to find little piglets rooting the ground.

Said fat mother pig half hid in the mud, "Come on, jump in, "A mud bath feels g-o-o-d!"

"Baa-a-a," said a white lamb, "My fleece is quite warm. When I am a big sheep, please, shear it for yarn."

The farm bell then tolled. "It's time to go eat," said Grandfather, scraping the mud from his feet.

"There'll be fresh bread, fresh butter, fresh milk, and sweet jam, hot soup with big dumplings, and smoke house cured ham."

Outside the window,
a ruckus began.
She sprang up to see,
and there from the barn:

Brown Cow, Old Daisy,
and from the pig pen,
the piglets, their mother,
plus rooster and hen.

Also, the goslings
with their mother goose,
the ducklings, the rabbit,
and lamb with white fleece.

Such baa-a-a-ing, such
mooing, such oinking,
such snort, such
peeping, such clucking,
such crowing...

All
  sounding
    together
     "We're glad
        that you've come to

THE BIG YELLOW HOUSE
ON
GRANDFATHER'S FARM."

And lest we forget,
the little field mouse
scurrying to get
to Grandfather's house
in time to add squeaking
to all of the din!

That, dear reader,
is where I shall end.

About the Author

In 1932, a night's trip by train, a big house painted yellow, and a German-speaking grandfather and a Czech-speaking grandmother, changed the course of life for author Dr. Agnes Evans Gish, then five. Her vivid memory of the occasion inspired her latest book *The Big Yellow House on Grandfather's Farm*, written with the adult readers in mind, but meant to be shared with children. Dr. Gish is also an author of three historical books, *The Sweet Springs of Western Virginia* (Heritage Books, 2007), *Virginia Taverns, Ordinaries, and Coffee Houses* (Heritage Books, 2005), and *Hobson's Chapel* (Deitz Press, 1997). She also published numerous newspaper and magazine articles such as "A place of considerable trade for its size" *Virginia Cavalcade* (Vol. 50, Number 2, Spring 2001) and "A Victorian Parlor Piano" *Antiques & Collecting Magazine* (1996).

Dr. Gish holds degrees from the College of Notre Dame of Maryland, Virginia Commonwealth University, and obtained a Doctorate of Education from the University of Northern Colorado.

She now resides at Knollwood, a military retirement community located in Washington, D.C., where, at the age of ninety, she continues to write, paint and direct the Knollwood Singers' annual creative musical productions.

www.ingramcontent.com/pod-product-compliance
Lightning Source LLC
Chambersburg PA
CBHW041645220426

43662CB00004B/60